# Barbecue Cooking

ROGER HICKS

# A QUINTET BOOK

ISBN: 0–7858–0506–0

This book was designed and produced by
Quintet Publishing Limited

Creative Director: Peter Bridgewater
Art Director: Ian Hunt
Designer: Michael Morey
Editor: Caroline Beattie
Photographers: Steve Alley, Amber Wisdom
Jacket Design: Nik Morley

Typeset in Great Britain by
Central Southern Typesetters, Eastbourne

Produced in Australia by Griffin Colour

Published by Chartwell Books
A Division of Book Sales, Inc.
P.O. Box 7100
Edison, New Jersey 08818–7100

The Publishers would like to thank
Weber-Stephen Products Co. for the use of the
barbecue pictures on pages 6, 7 & 8

# Contents

**B**arbecue cooking is unique, both in the flavours it produces and in the cooking techniques that are used. These can often reflect the character of the cook: large chunks of meat, raw on the inside, charred on the outside, and washed down with strong drink for those with hearty appetites, or a delicate chicken wing for the socialite.

The devotee of junk food can load up on prepared meat and poultry full of sulphites and preservatives, seasoned with a little synthetic 'liquid smoke', while the lover of good food, at whom this book is aimed, can prepare an extraordinary range of dishes, cooked with a variety of barbecue techniques or with a mixture of conventional and barbecue cooking methods, whether boiling, microwaving or steaming.

If you want to explore the full potential of a barbecue, it is a good idea not to have too many fixed ideas. Many people refuse to use aluminium foil when they are cooking on a barbecue, with the result that the wings and legs of chicken, and the small bones of some chops, are hopelessly charred long before the rest of the meat is cooked. Others believe that a barbecue isn't ready to use unless the temperature is sufficiently intense to blister unprotected skin (and indeed paintwork) an arm's length away: their penalty is food that is burned on the outside, and raw on the inside. It is *much* easier to cook large pieces of meat if your barbecue can be covered: trying to cook a rib roast on a simple *hibachi* is possible, but it involves a lot of hard work and there is a considerable risk of flare-ups, charring, and general lack of success.

Having said all this, it is almost impossible for any barbecue cookery book to cover all the ways of cooking that are known as 'barbecue'. For example, digging a pit and lining it with *maguey* leaves in order to cook a whole young goat requires a large garden, *maguey* leaves and whole young goats, which is likely to eliminate many readers. The same goes for spit-roasting whole oxen – a process which, incidentally, can take two or three *days*, and so should not be undertaken lightly. So what, then, is 'barbecue'?

At its most basic, it is cooking out of doors, using burning charcoal or wood to create a smoky flavour. While it is possible to use a barbecue in a well-ventilated garage (with the door open, and well away from inflammable materials), it isn't the same. Likewise, although there are quick, convenient gas barbecues, they don't make real barbecue-flavoured food unless you add water-soaked wood-chips to create the smoke – and soaked wood-chips wrapped in aluminium foil ain't the same as playing with fire!

Why do it? The food tastes good; it's a great opportunity for entertaining friends; it's surprisingly easy, and informal; it's a welcome change from the kitchen, especially in hot weather; and best of all, it's just plain *fun*.

## Food to Barbecue

You can cook almost anything on a barbecue, and it will usually taste good. The question is, how much of your cooking do you *want* to do on a barbecue? There are recipes for bread and apple pies, but apart from the tang from the smoke, there really isn't any point for those in using anything other than a conventional oven. The same goes for frying or boiling on the barbecue: if you are at home, it's generally easier to do this sort of thing on the stove.

On the other hand, there are many things you can cook on a barbecue that are quite unexpected – and indeed, some of the methods are unexpected, too. How about onions or baby pumpkins roasted in the coals? Or baked apples cooked in aluminium foil? Or combining steaming and smoking in a covered barbecue to produce fish that far surpasses the products of the commercial smokers.

For most people, barbecue means simply-cooked meat or chicken, often in the form of hamburgers or sausages. There are, however, many other ways to enjoy barbecued meat, especially if you explore international cuisines. Both Greece and India make versions of meatball kebabs; from East Asia comes satay, tiny kebabs on bamboo skewers, served with a peanut sauce; Tex-Mex cooking, from the southern borders of the United States, gives us *fajitas*; in Portugal, fresh sardines are grilled whole.

Even if you confine yourself to a single type of food, the sausage, there is an extraordinary variety available, including: The North American frankfurter (or regional variants such as the 'red hot' and 'white hot'); the Portuguese *linguica*; the Spanish or Mexican *chorizo*; the British 'banger'; the Cornish 'hog's pudding'; the German *Weisswurst*, *Blutwurst* or *Knackwurst* (among many others); the French *andouilles* and *saucissons secs;* Italian *mortadella* . . . The list is tremendous.

LEFT Steak is probably the food that is most often barbecued.

BELOW Korean-style beef, cut into strips and marinated before being grilled on a fierce heat.

LEFT Sausages are very popular for barbecuing; shown here are *Knackwurst* and *Bratwurst*.

The drawback to this admirably simple and indeed genuinely stone-age approach, though, is that the cook is also likely to be lightly barbecued. Also, the arms get tired. And what is more, digging large pits and filling them with burning oak is not calculated to improve a well-kept lawn, hence the other types of barbecue.

One of the simplest is the Japanese *hibachi*, made of cast iron. The fire-grate is situated about half-way up the *hibachi's* body, and the grill or grid can be adjusted by wedging it into one of three notches. The

Barbecue food has its own terminology. 'Spare ribs' are actually *spar* ribs, cooked on a stick or spar; and the unlikely-sounding 'buffalo wings' are actually chicken wings cooked in a style that originated in Buffalo, New York – which does not improve them much, as they remain bony, gristly, and messy, like all chicken wings.

Chicken wings, or the tiny bits of meat on *satay*, are a little out of the mainstream of 'real' barbecues, however. In Western Europe and the United States, barbecue cooking has a long and fairly straightforward history, often associated with cowboys, pirates and other hard-working if unconventional men. Not surprisingly, it is generally hearty fare. It can also be quite cheap. Sausages rarely cost much; chicken is no longer reserved for the rich; and cheap cuts of meat, if properly marinated and then barbecued, can be absolutely delicious. In the United States, the price of skirt steak (for *fajitas*) is ridiculously high, but in many other countries, this American delicacy can be bought for next to nothing.

## Barbecue Grills

The earliest barbecues were mostly pits dug in the ground, and the term 'barbecue pit' or 'oak-pit cooked' survives in much of the United States to this day. The simplest way to cook a piece of meat over a barbecue pit was to peel a green twig or small branch, impale the food on it, and hold it close enough to the coals to cook, but far enough away that it did not actually catch fire.

ABOVE A kettle barbecue fitted with a motor-driven rotisserie ensures even cooking for a fowl or a bulky cut of meat.

LEFT and RIGHT Variations on a theme: a basic barbecue that can be used open or covered (ABOVE LEFT) or with the cover as a shield on a windy day (LEFT). Barbecues with wheels make moving them much easier (RIGHT).

heat can further be controlled by means of sliding air-vents on the front: more air means more heat. You can do an astonishing amount of cooking with a *hibachi*, which is also very economical when it comes to fuel. It's a great barbecue for a couple, and it can feed four at a push (or with the right food), although it's not suitable for a party.

Slightly larger is the open grill: a round or square fire-pan, with a wire grill that can be raised or lowered either continuously, or on a ratchet. The principle is much the same as the *hibachi*, but because the open grill is usually bigger, you can control heat by positioning the coals so that some areas are hotter than others, as well as by opening or closing the air vents and raising or lowering the grill. This is essential if you want to cook by indirect heat: if you are cooking a large piece of meat, it is easiest to have a drip-pan (made of aluminium foil) underneath, to avoid flare-ups, and to use coals banked around the drip-pan to provide the heat.

If you add a cover to an open grill, you increase its versatility considerably. In effect, you create a sort of oven, so you can use lower heat for longer periods, and cook larger pieces of meat more easily and evenly. Even a partial hood can make a considerable difference, as it stops the food that is away from the fire from cooling too quickly. If you are cooking a large piece of meat, such as a rib of beef, you will need to turn it far less often if you have a covered grill.

Both open and covered grills can be used with an accessory spit for rotisserie cooking. Spits, spit baskets and tumble baskets are just some of the barbecue accessories.

The most complicated of all domestic barbecues is the steamer kettle. This is a large covered barbecue with an additional pan for water positioned just above the fire-grate. The idea is that the steam helps to cook the meat, resulting in a juicy, moist cut that is thoroughly permeated with the aromatic smell of the wood or charcoal. Most steamer kettles can also be used as plain grills, by removing the water pan and replacing it with the fire-pan.

When you choose a barbecue, consider the size you need; what sort of food you want to cook; when and where you want to cook; and the practicalities of maintenance and storage.

You can always cook small quantities of food on a large barbecue, but cooking large quantities of food on a small barbecue is hard work. On the other hand, a small barbecue uses less fuel and is ready for use faster. If you want to cook large cuts or whole fowl, a covered barbecue is highly desirable; a half-cover with a spit is the only convenient alternative.

In summer, in a sheltered corner, almost any barbecue is fun; but on a windy day, a cover or wind-shield is virtually essential. On a crisp, clear day in autumn or even winter, a cook-out can still be fun, but you need a covered barbecue if the meat is not to go stone-cold on one side while it is cooking on the other.

High-quality (which usually means expensive) barbecues are generally easier to keep clean than cheap ones. The drawbacks of rust are aesthetic rather than culinary, although a really cheap barbecue that is kept outdoors can literally rust to pieces. Porcelain (vitreous enamel) and stainless steel models will cost more than those finished with paint and chrome, but they will last better too.

A big barbecue also has to have a home: make sure that you have room for it somewhere, be it in your garage or your garden shed.

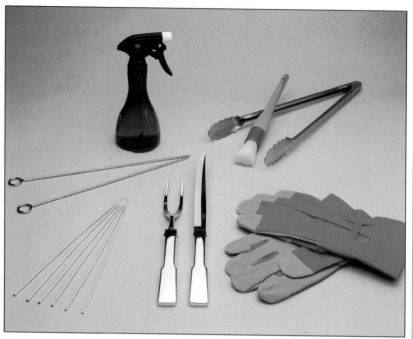

ABOVE Some of the tools for barbecuing; from top left, clockwise: tongs and a basting brush, a water sprayer, skewers (both metal and bamboo), a carving fork and knife, and heavy-duty gloves.

LEFT The ultimate barbecue/smoker, which can be used to smoke a turkey and a ham simultaneously.

# Tools and Accessories

Although you won't need many complicated tools for your barbecue, a pair of long-handled metal tongs at the very least will make it easier to manipulate the food, and will not cause loss of juices in the same way as a large, stout knife or even a meat-fork. As you learn more about barbecues, and decide on what and how you want to cook, you will evolve your own preferences; but the following 'star-rated' guide to accessories should be useful if you are just starting to take barbecues seriously. Three stars means 'must have'; two stars, either that something is essential only for some kinds of cookery, or that it is useful but not essential in other kinds; and one star means that you shouldn't throw it away if you receive it as a present, but that it's not worth rushing out and buying.

ALUMINIUM FOIL*** This offends some purists, but it's useful stuff. Wrap around chicken wings and other small parts of larger cuts to avoid charring. Also use as a parcel-wrap for some kinds of fish and vegetable cooking, on the grill or in the coals.

You can also use aluminium foil to make drip pans wind shields and saucepans, and you can use it to keep cooked food warm.

BASTING BRUSH*** You can survive without this, provided you never want to do any basting (moistening your meat, chicken or fish with the cooking juices);

RIGHT Use a basting brush to top up the sauce.

BELOW A complete barbecued meal: corn served with a sausage, chicken cooked in foil, grilled pineapple and salad.

you can do a surprising amount of cooking without it. Buy one with a long, stainless steel wire handle – or better still, buy a couple.

**DRIP TRAYS ••** If you want to cook large cuts, as already mentioned, put a drip tray under the meat or poultry and bank the coals around the edge. Disposable aluminium trays are ideal, although you can use cheap non-disposable cookware, or make the drip tray yourself from foil.

**FORK ••** A useful companion to tongs, but not essential. A heavy meat-carving fork is more useful than small cocktail forks with wooden handles and long metal rods terminating in a little fork: they are hardly big enough to pick up a large prawn.

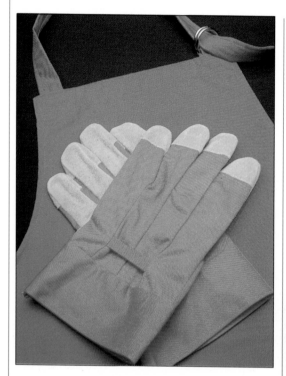

before use as they will slip through the food easier, and won't burn as fast. They won't burn at all if you are careful.

SPATULA** A metal spatula or fish slice is once again an adjunct to the tongs (below), and not essential. It does make it easier to cook hamburgers, though.

SPIT/ROTISSERIE** Once you have one of these, you'll use it continuously; if you don't, however, you'll probably never miss it.

SPIT BASKET* Similar to a grill basket, this is used on the spit.

TONGS*** Like the gloves, these are absolutely

GLOVES*** These are essential, and although purpose-made barbecue gloves are all very well, gardening gloves are safer, more comfortable, and last infinitely longer. Welder's gloves are another alternative.

GRILL BASKET* A wire mesh basket which opens like a book can be useful if you want to cook whole, delicate fish or anything else that is likely to fall apart when cooked.

MEAT THERMOMETER* These are no substitute for experience, and are never very accurate anyway. The only real use for them is to help you gain experience in cooking times.

POKER** You can rearrange the coals with almost anything, but a metal poker or rake is useful. Alternatively, keep a separate pair of tongs (see below) for adding and moving coals.

RACK* Like a grill basket, this sits on the grill and holds things in place. It is moderately useful for roasts, which otherwise tend to be difficult to rotate evenly.

SKEWERS** Long metal skewers are essential for most kinds of kebabs (kabobs). Stainless steel is far and away the best choice for most purposes, although short bamboo skewers are used in some kinds of cooking, notably *satay*. Soak these in water

essential. Go for the spring-loaded, stainless steel variety, as these give a much stronger and more secure grip than the scissor-type, and are much easier to use. As already mentioned, a second set of tongs is useful for adding fuel and rearranging the fire.

TUMBLE BASKET* This fits onto the spit, and is used for tumble-roasting chicken portions and (possibly) some kinds of sausage.

WATER-SPRAYER** Used to suppress flare-ups, a water-sprayer is essential if you want to cook large cuts or fatty meat. The choice of sprayer varies widely, and while some cooks like an ordinary water-pistol (squirt-gun), others use a well-cleaned squeeze-type detergent bottle, and yet others prefer a gardener's misting spray.

## Fuel

There are four types of barbecue fuel, each of which has its own advantages and disadvantages, and each of which affects the flavour of the food in a different way. They are wood, charcoal, charcoal briquettes, and gas.

Wood is still preferred by many people for both the flavour and the aroma of the wood smoke. Well-dried hardwoods are the most usual choice, as many soft-woods add unwanted resinous flavours to the food – although if you like retsina (Greek wine flavoured with pine-resin), you might like to try cooking with pine chips. It is, apparently, very good for some kinds of fish. The most usual wood employed is oak, closely followed by hickory, but you can use almost any type. Apple and pear wood are well regarded, and the roots of old grapevines are said to make a good fuel, although it is hard to find anyone who has actually used them, so this may be just a piece of barbecue folklore. Mesquite, which is often used after it has been turned into charcoal, is not good for a fire: it crackles and spits alarmingly, and was described by one enthusiastic barbecuer as being like something out of a science fiction movie.

Charcoal has almost as long a history as wood. It produces a much fiercer heat, and the coals are longer lasting, so it requires less attention and is more versatile. It is possible to find with different flavours: the distinctive smell and taste of mesquite is almost compulsory in the American South-west, for example.

If you buy 'real' charcoal (as distinct from the briquettes, described below), it usually comes in lumps of widely varying size. Building a fire from

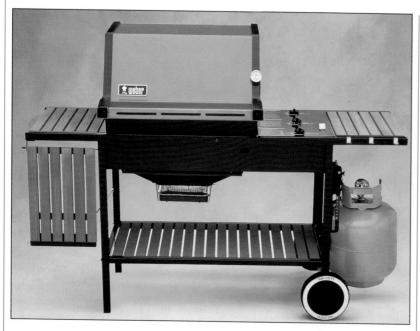

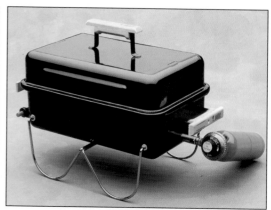

LEFT A sophisticated gas barbecue with temperature controls and space for keeping the food warm once it has been cooked.

ABOVE A more basic gas barbecue which has the added advantage of being portable.

these is quite an art, and it is generally easiest to smash the largest and least manageable lumps with a hammer and chisel before you use them.

Charcoal briquettes, according to one legend, were invented by the Ford Motor Company to use up the sawdust that was left over from making the floorboards of the Model T. Whether this is true or not, they are probably the most popular and convenient of barbecue fuels. One problem with briquettes, however, is that some brands impart a faint chemical taste to the food; this comes from the 'mastic' that is used to bind the powdered charcoal. You can't really taste it if you drown the food in sugary commercial barbecue sauce (which tastes like a refinery by-product anyway), but if you have spent hours preparing delicately marinated food, it is worth remembering. For this reason, those who care passionately about barbecues rarely use them. If they do, they test

several different brands until they find one which cooks like real charcoal; as some brands use much more petrochemical mastic binder than others. In addition to 'plain vanilla' briquettes, you can also get briquettes with a touch of mesquite, and even briquettes made from old Jack Daniels whiskey barrels!

In the case of gas barbecues, the 'coals' are actually lumps of inert rock which glow just like barbecue coals but have no flavour of their own to give to the food. The barbecues use propane or butane gas to heat them, but you can add flavour by throwing wood chips onto the coals. The recommended approach is to soak the chips (be they apple, hickory or oak) in water and wrap them in aluminium foil (so that the ash doesn't fall through the fake coals) before adding them to the fire. Although gas barbecues are easy to use and fire up quickly, in the eyes of many barbecue-lovers they are totally unacceptable.

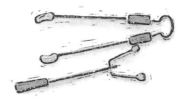

## Ingredients and Techniques

All too often, barbecuing is seen as an 'easy option' for the cook. While it is true that the sheer fun of barbecuing can make even indifferent food taste good, it is also true that a little more time, effort and (sometimes) money can make an enormous difference to the quality of your barbecuing.

Some kinds of barbecue cooking are unexpectedly easy – steaks, for example, or even quite large cuts of meat – whereas others are unexpectedly difficult. Hamburgers seem easy, but *good* hamburgers are another matter. Practice is essential to develop the mixture of experience and knowledge that you need in order to become a really good barbecue cook.

Pay attention when you are cooking. Barbecue temperatures are not easily controllable, and unlike roasting meat in an oven, barbecuing is not a "set it and forget it" process. Take both interest and pride in what you are doing.

Most importantly, choose your ingredients carefully. Good meat can be cooked simply, but cheap meat requires help. There is plenty of information about both in here. If you want to take short-cuts – garlic powder instead of fresh cloves, ground ginger instead of freshly-chopped ginger root – by all means do, but the more care you put into the preparation, the finer the results.

**BEER** Beer and barbecues are inseparable to many people, but instead of drinking generic 'maltade', American readers might care to try some of the products of their own smaller breweries, which have vastly more flavour, or to drink imported beer.

**EXOTIC INGREDIENTS** From time to time, recipes in this book call for unusual ingredients such as sesame oil or *mirin* (cooking sake). Substitutes are suggested, but the real thing will always taste better. Unless you live in the back of beyond, most ingredients will be available from a speciality or ethnic shop near you.

**GARLIC** A head of fresh garlic costs very little, and will keep for a long time (completely odourlessly) in the refrigerator.

**GINGER** Ginger root is readily available in many supermarkets and in most oriental, Indian and other ethnic speciality shops. Skinned and grated or finely chopped, it is infinitely superior to and in fact quite different from dried, powdered ginger. It also keeps well in the refrigerator.

**HERBS** Fresh herbs are best, but dried herbs can also be excellent, provided they have not been on your shelf too long. Dried herbs should be strongly aromatic when you rub them in your fingers, not dusty and musty.

ABOVE A tableful of barbecue ingredients ready for a cookout, plus ingredients to serve before and with the meal.

ABOVE To get the most out of your barbecue, prepare the fuel, the ingredients and accompaniments well in advance.

PEPPER Generally use fresh-ground black pepper, from a pepper-mill, and for marinades in which the meat will rest for many hours, use whole black peppercorns. Ready-ground black pepper is a poor substitute, and ready-ground white pepper is no substitute at all.

WINE You don't need *grands crus* for barbecues, but hearty, drinkable wines (reds in particular) can greatly improve a meal. California 'jug' wines, Eastern European wines or cheap, sparkling wines are ideal.

## Temperatures

Throughout this book, the following descriptions of temperature are used. Holding your hand above the coals at grill height (remove the grill first!), count how many seconds you can stand it. Unless you are unusually slow on the uptake, heat ratings are (approximately):

| | |
|---|---|
| 5 seconds | Low |
| 4 seconds | Low-medium |
| 3 seconds | Medium-hot |
| 2 seconds | Hot |
| Can't do it | Fierce |

Increase the heat by opening the air vents, pushing the coals closer together, or lowering the grill.

MUSTARD Mustard powder tastes completely different to prepared mustard, and which one you choose will depend on what you are preparing. Sweet, mild American mustard is great for burgers, but is not much use for mixing sauces; coarse-milled Dijon mustard is excellent with sausages.

OIL Olive oil tastes good, and is good for you. The strongest flavour comes from Greek 'extra virgin' olive oil (taken from the first pressing of the olives), and the best Italian, Spanish and even French oils are equally good. Second-pressing oil is weaker in flavour and lighter in colour, and 'pomace oil', extracted from the third pressing with the help of steam, is all but tasteless. Other good oils include walnut and grapeseed, and safflower and peanut oils are more appropriate for South-east Asian food, where olive oil is not authentic, or for blander food. Sesame oil has a unique hot, spicy flavour, whereas corn oil is barely adequate for frying: its only virtue is that it is cheap.

## Quantities

Throughout this book, quantities are given in metric, US and Imperial (English) measures. The more eagle-eyed readers will note that the equivalents are not always absolutely precise, and it is worth noting that measuring dry ingredients by the cup can be inaccurate: a lot depends on how tightly you pack the ingredients, how finely they are chopped, and so forth. Although the 'standard cup' is 8 fluid ounces, the American standard tablespoon is 15 ml or ½ fl oz, while the Australian standard tablespoon is 20 ml.

None of this is very important. Cooking is not a precise science, and you should always reckon that a recipe may need 'fine tuning'. This is particularly true when using garlic: quantities suggested in this book are on the low side, but they may often be doubled (or more) by garlic lovers. Similarly, ginger, sugar, salt and pepper can also be varied within very wide limits.

## WHITE WINE MARINADE

*1½ cups / 330 ml / 12 fl oz dry white wine*

*½ cup / 110 ml / 4 fl oz lemon or lime juice*

*1 tsp dry mustard*

*salt and pepper*

Use for fish, 12–48 hours.
 Add olive oil to taste for dry fish.

## BEER MARINADE

*1½ cups / 330 ml / 12 fl oz beer (1 can)*

*2 tbs cider or wine vinegar*

*½ cup / 110 ml / 4 fl oz olive oil*

*1 small onion, thinly sliced*

*2 garlic cloves, finely chopped*

*salt and pepper*

Use for beef, 8–48 hours.
 Ideally, use beer you can actually *taste*, such as Guinness, Anchor Porter or Bass, for example.

## RED WINE MARINADE

*1¼ cups / 280 ml / 10 fl oz red wine*

*⅔ cup / 150 ml / 5½ fl oz olive oil*

*1 small onion, finely chopped*

*2 garlic cloves, finely chopped*

*salt and pepper*

Use for beef, 12–48 hours.

## TERIYAKI

*1 cup / 225 ml / 8 fl oz soy sauce*

*⅔ cup / 150 ml / 5½ fl oz cooking sake (mirin)*

*⅓ cup / 75 ml / 3 fl oz vinegar*

*2 tbsp sesame oil*

*2 garlic cloves, finely chopped*

*1 tsp ginger root, chopped fine*

*salt and pepper*

Use with any meat, chicken or seafood, for 2 hrs to overnight.
 If you can't get cooking sake, use regular sake or sherry plus one-third of its own volume of sugar. Sesame oil, which is hot and spicy, is available in oriental shops. Ground ginger may be substituted for fresh chopped ginger, but is very inferior.

ABOVE White wine marinade is delicately flavoured enough to be used with fish.

## T A N D O O R I

| |
|---|
| *4 small dried red chillies* |
| *2 tbsp coriander seeds* |
| *1½ tbsp turmeric powder* |
| *2 tsp garam masala* |
| *6 garlic cloves, crushed* |
| *1 medium onion, chopped* |
| *½ oz / 15 g / ½ oz root ginger, grated* |
| *2 tbsp lemon juice* |
| *2 tsp salt* |

Grind together all the ingredients, except the salt and lemon juice, to make a smooth paste. Add the salt and lemon juice. Use either as a brushing sauce for chicken grilled conventionally, or as a marinade (rubbed onto the skin of the chicken) and then cook the chicken in foil.

## B E E R - C H I L L I - H O R S E R A D I S H

| |
|---|
| *⅓ cup / 75 ml / 3 fl oz beer* |
| *½ cup / 110 ml / 4 fl oz chilli sauce* |
| *2 tbsp grated horseradish* |
| *1 tbsp very finely chopped onion* |
| *½ tsp sugar* |
| *½ tsp salt* |
| *¼ tsp ground black pepper* |
| *¼ tsp dry mustard* |

This requires no cooking; just mix, and use on beef. Canned chilli sauce can be used for this mixture as once it's been grilled, no-one will know that it wasn't home made!

## P I N E A P P L E

| |
|---|
| *8 oz / 225 gm / ½ lb can crushed pineapple* |
| *2 tsp cornflour (cornstarch)* |
| *3 tbsp honey* |
| *2 tbsp soy sauce* |
| *2 tbsp cider vinegar* |

Combine the pineapple and the cornflour in a saucepan and add the other ingredients. Heat for 5 minutes, stirring constantly. Use for chicken and pork.

## G E N E R I C   B A R B E C U E   S A U C E

| |
|---|
| *1¼ cups / 225 g / 8 oz tomato purée (sauce)* |
| *⅓ cup / 75 ml / 3 fl oz vinegar* |
| *⅓ cup / 100 g / 3 oz brown sugar* |
| *1 medium onion, chopped* |
| *1–4 garlic cloves, finely chopped* |
| *1 tbsp chilli powder* |
| *2 tbsp American (mild) mustard* |

Mix all the ingredients bring to the boil and simmer for 5 minutes. This recipe is authentically American, but non-Americans may care to reduce the sugar and use 1 tbsp of dry mustard.

## A P R I C O T - G I N G E R

| |
|---|
| *¾ cup / 225 g / 8 oz apricot preserve* |
| *2 tbsp cider vinegar* |
| *2 tbsp melted butter* |
| *1 tsp root ginger, finely chopped* |

This may be a little sweet for some tastes, but substituting fresh apricots which are then puréed in a food processor results in a remarkable sauce. It requires no cooking: just mix and use.

ABOVE Pineapple sauce is popular with pork and chicken, as are grilled pineapple rings.

# Butters

If you are not too worried either about cholesterol or about keeping kosher, flavoured butters are a traditional accompaniment to many barbecued dishes. Soften the butter (to room temperature) before trying to mix any of the following, which are based on ½ cup / 4 oz / 110 g of butter.

ANCHOVY BUTTER Chop or shred two or three anchovy fillets (or to taste – it could be a whole can!) and pound well with the butter.

GARLIC BUTTER Add 1 tsp each of finely chopped parsley and garlic ground in a pestle and mortar. Use with steak, bread and shrimp.

HERB BUTTER Add 2 tbsp each of finely chopped spring (green) onions and parsley, and ½ tsp tarragon leaves. Use with chicken, fish and vegetables.

HERB AND CHEESE BUTTER Add 3 tbsp grated Parmesan cheese, 1 tbsp finely chopped parsley, ½ tsp basil leaves and 1 clove garlic crushed and chopped. Use with vegetables.

BLUE CHEESE BUTTER Add ⅓ cup / 2 oz / 60 g crumbled blue cheese, 1 tbsp sliced spring (green) onions with tops and 1 clove garlic, crushed and chopped. Use with beef.

MUSTARD BUTTER Add 2 heaped tbsp Dijon mustard, 1 tbsp sliced spring (green) onions with tops and 1 clove garlic, crushed and chopped. Use with beef or poultry.

Seasoned butters may be served at room temperature, or melted for brushing.

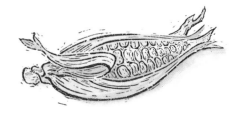

Basic grilling is very much like cooking over a camp fire, and is suitable only for fairly small pieces of meat. Normally, you sear the meat over a fierce heat, then use a lower temperature to complete the cooking.

The thicker the piece of meat, the longer it will take to cook all the way through; once it is more than about 2 in (5 cm) thick, it will take so long for the interior to cook thoroughly that you can no longer use a basic open-grill technique. The exception to this is beef – and then only if you and your guests like their beef very, very rare.

When you are grilling smaller pieces of meat (including hamburgers and chicken) it is important to avoid two things: charring and flare-ups. You can reduce both to a minimum by intelligent trimming, taking off any protruding, meatless bones or small flaps of carelessly cut meat. Bones will char, and small bits of meat will burn. Small, exposed areas that cannot be trimmed, such as chicken wings, and the bones which protrude from lamb chops, should be wrapped in aluminium foil to prevent charring.

Next, cut off all fat that is more than about ¼ in (6 cm) wide; as the meat is cooking, the fat will melt, and melted fat on the coals is what causes flare-ups. Do not try to remove *all* fat, as this will result in meat that is dry and tough: there has to be some fat for flavour and tenderness.

For fat remaining around the edge of the meat, you should cut through the fat to the meat – although not actually *into* the meat – to prevent the meat from curling. Both meat and fat contract slightly as they are cooked, but meat contracts to a greater extent, hence the curling.

One of the most important things you can do to ensure even cooking throughout is to have the meat (or anything else) at room temperature before you cook it. Take it out of the refrigerator an hour or two before you are ready to cook, and let it warm up. If you were not aware of this trick before, you will be amazed at how much easier it is to cook things from room temperature, and you will also find that they taste much better.

Before you start cooking, oil the grill to help pre-

BELOW A large steak which has been seared on one side and is now cooking more slowly on the other.

ABOVE Although large steaks are more usual for barbecues, small steaks are also delicious. Choose your cut carefully.

vent sticking – some people use spare fat trimmed from the meat.

## Steaks

Steaks and barbecues go extremely well together – and luckily, they are about the easiest thing in the world to barbecue to perfection. Crisp on the outside, tender in the middle, aromatic with the smoke of the barbecue – delicious!

In the United States in particular, the tendency is to serve massive steaks, – weighing at least 1 lb / 450 g and often 1¼ lb / 650 g. In part, this is because a steak *must* be big if it is to be cooked in the traditional barbecue manner; thinner steaks can be barbecued, but the effect is very different. A steak for barbecuing must be at least 1 in (2.5 cm) thick, and 2 in (5 cm) is by no means unusual.

While some cuts can conveniently be divided between two people, it is difficult to divide most steaks so that both people get a fair share of the good meat and the bone, fat, etc.

The best steaks for frying or grilling (broiling) are not necessarily the best for barbecuing. Fillet steak (filet), for example, is almost wasted on a barbecue. The delicate flavour of the meat is overwhelmed by the smoke, and the contrast in texture between the crisp outside and the tender inside is a little too great: the inside can seem mushy and flavourless. What is more, a fillet steak that is big enough to barbecue properly will be extremely expensive, and will better serve two or three people than one, as with *chateaubriand*, cut from the centre of the fillet. Small fillet steaks require enormous concentration if they are not to be overcooked.

The classic steaks for barbecuing are, therefore, T-bones and their close relatives, porterhouse and club (or Delmonico) steaks; rib steaks (*entrecôtes*); strip steaks (made from the non-fillet side of the T-bone or porterhouse, and also called New York Strip, or *contrefilet*); sirloin; and the rather tougher rump steak. A 'London Broil' (unknown in London, but popular in the United States) is or should be a thick piece of high-quality top rump. But these are not the only possibilities: the Far Western Tavern in Guadalupe (California), one of the world's great steak houses, has registered the name 'Bull's Eye' for a big steak taken from the eye or interior of the rib.

All of these steaks are best served plain-barbecued, with no marinating and no sauce, although some people like to dress them with butter (including flavoured butter) for serving. The smallest steaks that are normally served are 6 oz / 180 g, although a more usual small steak is about ½ lb / 225 g; ¾ lb / 350 g is a typical large steak in Britain, whereas 1 lb / 450 g is a Texas-style portion. All weights are uncooked: a steak typically loses 10–20 per cent of its weight during cooking, depending on how it is cooked and for how long.

For best results, sear one side over a high heat, and then finish cooking the other over a medium-to-low heat. Searing times are fairly consistent whether the steak is to be rare, medium, or well done.

The first table below is for high quality, tender steaks such as T-bone, porterhouse, and sirloin. For thicker 2 in (5 cm) steaks, use a slightly lower heat on the second side.

| THICKNESS | FIRST SIDE (High) | SECOND SIDE (Medium-low) |
|---|---|---|
| 1 in (2.5 cm) | 2–3 minutes | Rare: 2–3 minutes<br>Medium: 5–8 minutes<br>Well done: 10 minutes or more |
| 2 in (5 cm) | 4–6 minutes | Rare: 8–10 minutes<br>Medium: 12–15 minutes<br>Well done: 20 minutes or more |

To cook tougher cuts, first marinate the meat – a red wine marinade . Puncture the steak, both with and across the grain, using a sharp knife; this will help the marinade to penetrate. No cooking information is given for 'well-done' steaks here – they would be too tough. Slice the thicker steaks diagonally to serve.

| THICKNESS | FIRST SIDE (High) | SECOND SIDE (Medium-low) |
|---|---|---|
| 1 in (2.5 cm) | 5–6 minutes | Rare: 15 minutes<br>Medium: 20 minutes |
| 2 in (5 cm) | 8 minutes | Rare: 20 minutes<br>Medium: 23 minutes |

BELOW T-bone steak is rightly one of the favourites for barbecuing. It can be served with rice, salad and pita bread.

ABOVE Korean-style beef cooks very quickly and is often eaten just as fast!

# Korean Barbecue and Beef Teriyaki

In the Far East, beef is often barbecued in much thinner strips than in the West. This allows for very quick cooking on a surprisingly small grill: a *hibachi* is perfectly adequate for a dinner-party for four, and you can almost as easily feed six. For success, you will need a *very* sharp chopping knife to slice the meat; partially freezing it will make cutting very much easier.

## KOREAN BEEF

SERVES 4 – 6

*1 tbsp sesame seeds*

*1 cup spring (green) onions, finely chopped*

*2–4 garlic cloves, very finely chopped*

*¼ cup / 55 ml / 2 fl oz soy sauce*

*2 tbsp sugar*

*2 tbsp dry sherry or sake*

*2 tbsp peanut or sesame oil*

*1½ lb / 750 g / 1½ lb beef (chuck, round or sirloin) in a slice about 1 in (2.5 cm) thick*

Toast the sesame seeds in a heavy iron skillet, shaking frequently to avoid burning and popping, until golden. Grind the toasted seeds in a pestle and mortar or spice grinder. Mix thoroughly with the spring onions, garlic, soy sauce, sugar, wine and oil.

Slice the meat into strips about ¼ in (6 mm) thick. Add to the marinade, stirring to coat thoroughly. Marinate for an hour or two.

Over a high or even fierce heat, grill the strips until the meat is browned, but still rare – about 30 seconds to 1 minute per side.

In Korea, this would be served with *kimchi* (pickled salty cabbage, available at Korean stores), stir-fried bean sprouts and plain boiled rice. If you can't get *kimchi*, try a coleslaw or cucumber salad with vinegar dressing.

## BEEF TERIYAKI

Use the teriyaki sauce recipe for this dish. Teriyaki sauce straight from the bottle can be quite good, and you can add a little freshly chopped garlic to taste if you like.

For 4–6 people, you need 2–3 lb / 1–1.5 kg of beef. It need not be of outstanding quality: top round or chuck is fine, but it should be in a single slice, at least 1 in (2.5 cm) thick.

With the meat semi-frozen, cut strips as thin as you can, across the grain: ⅛ in (3 mm) is about right. The trick is to saw rapidly.

Soak bamboo skewers in water to avoid charring, and then thread the meat onto them. Pour the marinade over the skewered meat, and turn the sticks frequently to assure even coverage and penetration: 30 minutes of soaking is enough.

Grill over a hot or fierce fire for 3–4 minutes until the meat is browned but not dried out. Serve as an *hors d'oeuvres* (for up to 12 people) or with rice and vegetables cooked in the Japanese style.

LEFT Pork chops, which can be marinated for flavour or served with a sauce.

## Chops and Cutlets

The techniques used for cooking chops and cutlets are much the same as those for cooking steaks, although you have to make adjustments according to the type of meat used.

A chop or cutlet consists of a rib bone and the meat attached to it. For pork, it is normally called a chop; for lamb and veal, 'chop' and 'cutlet' are used interchangeably; and for venison, 'cutlet' or 'noisette' are the usual terms.

### PORK CHOPS

Hind loin chops are dryer than fore loin ones, and so are less suitable for barbecuing. Shoulder chops are the fattest, but have an excellent flavour. True chop-lovers would grill them unadorned, but you can both marinade them and use some kind of basting or barbecue sauce. With hind loin chops, this is probably a good idea. A cider marinade is ideal, or use one of the sweet marinades such as pineapple or cola.

Unlike steaks, pork chops are not seared, as it toughens them. Trim the fat and    cook a 1 in (2.5 cm) chop over a medium to low heat for 25–30 minutes, turning once. Thinner chops may be cooked in as little as 12–15 minutes: be careful to avoid over-cooking, or the meat will be tough. The meat is cooked when the juices run clear if you pierce the meat with a skewer or knife – but don't test it too often, or the meat will dry out.

Smoked chops cook faster than unsmoked chops: 1 in (2.5 cm) chop should be cooked in 15–20 minutes.

### LAMB CHOPS

Rib chops are distinguished by a long bone and a small 'nut' of lean meat surrounded by fat. You need to watch these carefully if they are not to be over-cooked, but they taste excellent. Middle neck cutlets are messier to eat – the meat extends to the bone – but are easier to cook. Loin chops are the easiest of all to cook, because they are usually biggest and thickest, and they have the most meat. The most impressive chops to look at are butterfly chops (two chops joined at the top) and are cooked in exactly the same way.

Cook over a medium heat: a chop 1 in (2.5 cm) thick should take 15 minutes or a little less, while thin chops can be cooked in 5–10 minutes. Watch them carefully and turn once.

Lamb chops can be eaten with the meat a little pink, although well-done lamb is less tough than well-done pork or beef. If you want to marinate the chops first, try the following marinade:

#### WHITE WINE/HONEY

| |
| --- |
| *1½ cups / 330 ml / 12 fl oz white wine* |
| *½ cup / 110 ml / 4 fl oz honey* |
| *2 tbsp vinegar* |
| *2 tsp fresh mint, chopped* |
| *1 garlic clove, crushed and chopped* |

Marinate for 4–24 hours.

# Sausages

Although it is possible to cook almost any sausage on the barbecue, it is a good idea to pre-cook fresh sausages and then to cook them by indirect heat over a drip pan. All sausages are fatty, and flare-ups are a virtual certainty if you do not take these precautions. With some cooked sausages, such as frankfurters, fat is not a problem, while others seem to contain almost as much fat as fresh sausages.

The best way to pre-cook fresh sausages is on the barbecue, very slowly, a long way above or to one side of the coals, and let the fat drip out and burn. The easiest way, however, is in the microwave. Prick the skins, and cook at one of the lower settings until the fat begins to run out (use a sloping 'bacon tray' for convenience). Alternatively, use the grill (broiler) in the oven, turning frequently. If you want to pre-cook them on the barbecue, you can also wrap them in aluminium foil with a couple of tablespoons of water, and allow to render for 10–15 minutes. But be careful when you unwrap them.

**BLACK PUDDING, BLUTWURST, BLOOD SAUSAGE** A cooked sausage which may be barbecued in slices 1–2 in (2.5 cm) long without very great risk of flare-up, although a drip tray is a better idea. Great for a hearty brunch. Takes 5–10 minutes over low heat.

**BOLOGNA** Cook as for black pudding, above.

**BRATWURST** Pre-cook, or buy ready-cooked bratwurst. Prick the skin, and cook over a drip tray.

**BRITISH 'BANGERS'** Prick skins and cook over a low heat until the fat has rendered out. They usually contain so much cereal that the rendering is a slow process. These taste surprisingly good if they are left to go cold after they are fully cooked.

ABOVE Sausages vary from one country to another, so it is always worth looking in delicatessens and supermarkets for the most interesting selection.

LEFT Sausages are good with pasta salad, potato salad or plain vegetables cooked in the embers.

LEFT Linguica, being a pork sausage, needs thorough cooking.

CHORIZO Pre-cook these. Thin chorizo can be cooked in the same way as British sausages (above), but thick chorizo should be split lengthways with a knife (though not all the way through) and grilled over a low heat for 10–20 minutes.

FRANKFURTERS Ideally, these should be smoked in a water-smoker until they are hot, then finished on the grill. In practice, they can be grilled straight from the can, without drip trays or any other precautions, in well under 10 minutes. Turn frequently. The same goes for 'red-hots' and 'white-hots', which are regional variants with a skin.

HOG'S PUDDING A rare delicacy, available mainly in Cornwall and the West Country in Britain. Excellent if grilled like black pudding (see above).

LINGUICA (Portuguese pork sausage) Cook as for thick chorizo, above.

POLISH SMOKED SAUSAGE Cook as for thick chorizo.

SALAMI Dry sausages of all kinds can be cooked. They will render out a lot of fat, and become very crumbly, but the flavour is excellent. Cook as for black pudding, above.

WEISSWURST This is normally boiled, but a whole boiled weisswurst can be finished on the barbecue and will taste all the better for it. Cook briefly from hot, turning often.

To accompany sausages, consider sauerkraut, German potato salad, and potato pancakes.

# Burgers

*Nothing* is easier to make than a hamburger, but cooking them successfully is another matter.

If you want to save calories, use lean (22 per cent fat) mince (ground beef) but do not be tempted to use extra lean (15 per cent) mince (ground beef). Much of the fat will render out anyway, and the extra lean meat can be rather dry. The smallest hamburgers that can conveniently be barbecued are 4 oz / 110 g, but 6 oz / 180 g or 8 oz / 225 g are better. Anything much larger can be awkward to keep in one piece, and will certainly be harder to cook evenly. Once again, all weights are before cooking: a hamburger can lose up to 25 per cent of its weight during the cooking process, through loss of moisture and fat.

For a first-class basic hamburger, you need add absolutely nothing to the meat: it's the meat, the whole meat, and nothing but the meat. You do *not* need egg, which will spoil the flavour. Shape the meat (at room temperature) into patties that are about 1 in (2.5 cm) thick. Handle the hamburger as little as possible – this will help to keep it tender – before cooking it as follows:

| THICKNESS | FIRST SIDE (High) | SECOND SIDE (Medium-low) |
|---|---|---|
| *1 in (2.5 cm)* | *2–4 minutes* | *Rare: 4–5 minutes*<br>*Medium: 6–8 minutes*<br>*Well done: 10–15 minutes* |

If you want to add barbecue sauce, the 'generic' is probably the most suitable.

Drop the burger on the (oiled) grill and brush the upper surface with sauce. When you flip the burger, brush the cooked side. For a patty melt, add the sliced cheese 2–5 minutes before cooking is complete: some cheeses melt faster than others!

## FLAVOURED HAMBURGERS

For flavoured burgers, try adding any or all of the following to the raw beef. Mix quickly, to avoid excessive handling:

tomato ketchup (catsup)
taco sauce
chopped onions
finely chopped garlic (don't overdo it!)
Worcestershire sauce
mustard
Salt
Freshly-ground black pepper

## STUFFED HAMBURGERS

You may also care to try stuffed hamburgers. Make the patties ½ in (1.3 cm) thick and between the two layers try any or all of the following. Seal the edges as best you can (don't use too much stuffing!) and cook as for a regular hamburger:

Cheese (Cheddar, mozzarella, or blue)
Cooked bacon
Chopped onion
Pickles
Peppers
Olives

## PRESENTATION

Whether plain, flavoured or stuffed hamburgers, the classic presentation is in a large, soft, tasteless hamburger bun which has to be toasted over the barbecue in order to impart any flavour or texture to it at all. But all kinds of other breads – French bread, sourdough rolls, muffins, bagels and even pumpernickel or croissants – can also be used.

Classic salad accompaniments are iceberg lettuce and tomato, and cucumber and sliced dill pickles are also usual. For onion, use thinly sliced red onion or chopped spring (green) onions for a milder flavour than raw white onion. Whereas in Britain fried onions are sometimes served with hamburgers, in the United States, they are more likely to be raw.

Other garnishes include sour cream; bottled or home-made chili con carne or pizza sauce; sliced olives; sliced avocado (very popular in California!); crispy-fried bacon; mustard; tomato ketchup (catsup); and many kinds of proprietary salad dressings.

BELOW Cucumber dill pickles are often served with hamburgers because of their sharp flavour.

ABOVE Barbecued chicken pieces are very tasty, especially with the addition of a flavoured butter.

## Chicken

Barbecuing is one of the very best (and easiest) ways of adding flavour to modern, bland, unexciting chicken (a problem you will not have if you can buy free range chickens). You can cook chicken pieces (legs, wings, quarters and halves) over either an open or a covered barbecue; the latter will give you more flavour and shorten the cooking time, and whole fowl are much easier to cook with an enclosed barbecue. If you are using a meat thermometer, look for an interior temperature of 185°F / 85°C.

### CHICKEN PIECES

Cook over a medium, direct heat with no drip tray. Turn every 10 minutes, basting from time to time with melted butter: herbs, such as oregano or sage, or garlic butter can be added for extra flavour. Sprinkle the chicken with salt and pepper before cooking, both to add flavour and to crisp the skin.

|  | Open Barbecue | Covered Barbecue |
|---|---|---|
| Breasts, boned | 12–15 minutes | 10–12 minutes |
| Wings, legs | 35–40 minutes | 30–35 minutes |
| Quarters | 40–50 minutes | 30–40 minutes |
| Halves | 1 hour or more | 45 minutes or more |

## WHOLE CHICKEN

Wipe the bird inside and out; do not stuff. Season with salt and pepper.

Truss carefully, and cover wingtips and leg ends with aluminium foil. Cook over medium, indirect heat (use a drip tray) in a covered barbecue. A middling-size chicken of 2½–3½ lb (1.25–1.6 kg) should cook in about 1¼–1½ hrs. Turn three or four times during that time.

For a faster-cooking, and arguably better-tasting, bird, take a heavy knife and split the bird along the backbone. Pull hard, cracking the breastbone, and flatten the chicken into a sort of 'butterfly' shape. Undercut the wing and leg joints slightly, to help the bird lie flat. Lean on the whole with the heel of your hand to flatten thoroughly, and slit the thigh to help it cook more evenly. Marinate in red wine marinade for at least a couple of hours. Grill over a medium, direct heat, skin side first, until it is golden and crispy, then place bone side downwards. Baste with olive oil, turning occasionally. The total cooking time with this method will be 35–45 minutes for an average-size chicken.

BELOW To prevent leg-ends and wing-tips burning, cover them in foil.

## PRE-COOKING

To save time, part-cook half and whole chickens in a microwave oven before barbecuing. Cook in the microwave for half of the oven manufacturer's recommended time and finish on the grill with half of the recommended times in this book.

# Other Poultry

Most types of poultry can be cooked on a spit . It may not have occurred to you, though, that it is perfectly possible to cook everything from a pigeon weighing under 1 lb / 450 g to a turkey that weighs 15–16 lb / 7 kg plus. You *must*, however, have a covered barbecue to cook anything other than the smallest fowl.

## TURKEY

Wipe and season the bird, inside and out. An 8 lb / 3½ kg turkey will serve 6–8 people, with leftovers; and a 15 lb / 7 kg turkey will serve 12–15.

ABOVE Cornish hen makes a good meal for two.

Cook over a medium heat with a drip tray underneath, turning every 15 minutes or so and basting with melted butter. As with chicken pieces, use herb or garlic butter for extra flavour. An 8 lb / 3½ kg bird should take 2–2½ hours, while a 15 lb / 7 kg bird will take at least 4 hours.

With birds of this size, though, the meat will continue to cook for 20–30 minutes after it is removed from the heat. You will get a juicier, better-baked turkey if you remove it from the heat a few minutes before it is fully cooked – when the meat thermometer shows 175°F / 80°C – and allow it to sit for 20 minutes for a small bird, 30 minutes for a big one. The meat thermometer will continue to rise until it shows the requisite 185°F / 85°C: when it does, the bird is ready to carve.

## PIGEON

Allow one whole pigeon per person. Wrap a slice of bacon around the breast and back – pigeons are not particularly fatty – and roast over a medium-high direct heat for 15–25 minutes, turning once. Unlike other whole fowl, you can cook pigeons with an open grill, but covered barbecues are quicker and give a better flavour.

## CORNISH GAME HEN

A small chicken, completely unknown in Cornwall, this is a popular dish in the United States. The nearest English (or Cornish) equivalent is a small spring chicken: whole hens typically weigh 1½ lb / 750 g. One hen can serve two people easily.

Cook for 25–30 minutes over medium heat, with a drip tray.

## TO COOK STUFFING

Use either a commercial stuffing mix, or make up your own favourite. Wrap in a double thickness of aluminium foil, and add between 1 tsp and 1 tbsp of extra water. Seal carefully and cook on the edge of the grill over a very low heat for at least 15–20 minutes.

Kabab, an Arabic word also found in Persian and Urdu, has been spelled in a wide variety of ways including 'cabob' and 'keebaub'. It is only quite recently that most of the English-speaking world has standardized on 'kebab', while Americans often settle for 'kabob'.

Although kebabs are found throughout the Near East, and indeed throughout the world, the Greeks (and for that matter, the Yugoslavs and Albanians) make some of the simplest: cubes of lamb or pork, cooked on a skewer, and served either with rice or in a pocket of pita bread (or pitta bread – again, the spelling isn't standardized) with a squeeze of lemon juice, a salad, and a couple of ferocious peppers.

## Greek Pork Kebabs

A couple of pounds (just under one kilo) of boned pork meat will make enough kebabs for 4–6 people if served with rice, or 6–8 if served with plenty of salad in pita bread. The meat is usually marinated for at least 1 hr in a mixture of lemon juice and oil: two or three parts of oil to one part of lemon juice is ideal. The marinade is also used for basting.

Shoulder of pork is traditional and economical, and tastes very good, but it may be a little fatty for some tastes. And although the loin is delicious and tender, it will require constant basting with a mixture of olive oil if it is not to become tough. So leg of pork is probably the best compromise: it·tastes good, and has enough fat to keep it juicy while still being high-quality meat.

Whichever cut you choose, dice it into cubes approximately 1¼ inches (3 cm) square, and thread these onto a skewer so that they are touching: you do not want any space between the pieces of meat. Marinate for at least 1 hr – overnight will do no harm, although a marinade with more oil and less lemon juice may be advisable (three-to-one instead of two-to-one).

Cook over a medium-low fire which extends somewhat beyond the meat on the kebab: cooking on a too-small grill tends to mean the meat in the middle will be cooked while the ends are not. If you only have a small barbecue, such as a *hibachi*, make very short stacks of meat on the skewer: 4 in (10 cm) of tight-packed meat is (just) sufficient for one pita filling, with salad.

Cook for at least 15 minutes, turning frequently unless you like rare pork: 20 minutes is about the upper limit.

## Greek Lamb Kebabs

The basic procedure is the same as for pork kebabs: again, shoulder is traditional, but leg is better. Cooking times are slightly shorter – perhaps 2 minutes less than for a similar sized skewer of pork.

### SERVING WITH PITA

Heat the pita bread for 15–30 seconds on each side: it should puff up and make it easy to slit for filling. The traditional Greek salad filling consists of shredded white cabbage with a dressing of olive oil and lemon juice, about three parts oil to one part of lemon juice. Add a couple of slices of tomato; 1 tbsp or so of diced cucumber; and a couple of thin slices of raw, or 1 tsp of chopped, onion. Give your guests the option of extra Greek peppers: Italian *pepperoncini* are an acceptable substitute, although they are not quite as good.

Put the salad in first; strip the meat off the skewer, into the pita; then lay a pepper over the top. Serve with wedges of lemon to squeeze over the meat.

Half a head of cabbage, two or three tomatoes, one cucumber and one medium onion should provide plenty of salad for four people.

### BARBECUE SAUCES

Although the Greeks would never use American-style barbecue sauces, there is no reason why you should not use them for the last 10 minutes or so of cooking, if you like them.

## Steak Kebabs

A basic steak (or beef) kebab – Basque-style, for example – is very much like a Greek-style kebab: the same 1¼ in (3 cm) cubes, with no other ingredients. Some people like to push the meat close together, like pork and lamb, while others prefer to leave a small space between the pieces, as this gives a larger area to crisp on the outside.

There is a major difference, however, in cooking times and temperatures. Steak kebabs are normally cooked over a medium-hot or even hot fire, and if the pieces of meat are separated instead of being pushed together, a rare kebab might be cooked for as little as 3–4 minutes over hot coals, being turned once a minute or more frequently. Even if the meat is pushed together, 10 minutes is as long as most people would want to cook a beef kebab over medium-hot coals.

ABOVE Steak kebabs are often served plain, though many people appreciate breads and salads with them.

Cut the meat smaller than you would for an all-meat kebab. Instead of a 1¼ in (3 cm) cube, try cutting squares that are 1¼ in (3 cm) on each side but only ½–¾ in (about 1.5 cm) thick.

Unless the meat is *very* thin – ¼ in (6 mm) or so – do not press moist vegetables close against it: the steam from the vegetables will keep the temperature too low to allow the meat to cook properly.

The best way to make a garnished kebab is probably with long, thin strips of meat. Begin with a piece of medium-quality steak about 1¼ in (3 cm) thick. Chill it to make cutting easier, and with a *very* sharp knife, slice off pieces ¼ in (6 mm) thick. Marinate to tenderize, using one of the marinades.

Weave the strips of meat accordion-style onto the skewer. Between the folds of the accordion, insert vegetables or even fruit: wedges of orange, pineapple, plaintain, cherry tomatoes, mushrooms (previously steamed for a minute or two), small stewing onions, or whatever you like.

Cook over medium coals for about 15 minutes.

What is more, steak kebabs are more often served with baked potatoes and beans or other vegetables, rather than with bulky breads and salads, so the quantities of meat required per person tend to be higher: ½ lb / 225 g of boneless beef (uncooked weight) per person is a reasonable minimum.

## GARNISHED KEBABS

In general, it is a good idea to avoid excessive cleverness or creativity when dealing with steak kebabs: those wonderful cookery-book pictures which show meat alternated with wedges of onion, cherry tomatoes, peppers and mushrooms are virtually impossible to cook, because all the ingredients cook at different rates. If you are determined to make this sort of kebab, note the following points:

Use only beef. The risk of undercooking pork is too great, though if you like underdone lamb, by all means consider that.

RIGHT Garnished kebabs take some preparation but are moist and tasty.

ABOVE Meatballs have the advantage that they can be flavoured in various ways before being cooked.

# Meatball Kebabs

The humble meatball takes amazingly well to being barbecued. The important thing is to suspend the skewers on some kind of rack, so that the meat does not touch the grill: if it does, it will probably stick, and the meatball is then likely to disintegrate as you try to pull it away. Here are two recipes, one which is relatively simple and is Greek, the other being a much subtler Indian dish.

## KEFETHES (GREEK)

### SERVES 8

| |
|---|
| ½ cup / 110 ml / 4 fl oz dry white wine |
| 1 cup / 225 ml / 8 fl oz water |
| ½ lb / 225 g / ½ lb stale bread |
| 2 or 3 medium onions, finely chopped |
| 2 lb / 900 g / 2 lb minced (ground) beef or veal |
| ½ lb / 225 g / ½ lb minced (ground) pork |
| 2 tbsp fresh chopped mint or spearmint |

Mix the wine and water; soak the bread in this. Parboil the onions for three minutes. Drain, and chop finely when cool. Mix all the ingredients together, and leave for at least 20 minutes for the flavours to blend.

Form into about three dozen sausage-shaped patties, and thread onto skewers. Cook over a medium

to low heat for at least 20 minutes, turning frequently and basting occasionally with olive oil or a mixture of olive oil and lemon juice, as for Greek-style kebabs

Serve with salad, garnished with fried potatoes. This is hearty food: a bottle of *retsina* (resinated Greek wine) is a good accompaniment.

## SEEKH KEBAB (INDIA)

### SERVES 6

| |
|---|
| 1½ lb / 750 gm / 1½ lb minced (ground) mutton or lamb |
| 1 tsp grated root ginger |
| 1 large onion, finely chopped |
| 4 tbsp / 25 g / 1 oz gram flour * |
| 1 fresh hot green chillies, chopped |
| 1 tsp green mango powder * |
| 1 tbsp salt |
| juice of half a lemon |
| 1 large egg |
| 2 tbsp chopped coriander leaves |
| ¼ cup / 60 g / 2 oz ghee (clarified butter) |

### SPICES

| |
|---|
| ½ tsp poppy seeds, roasted and ground |
| 1 tsp Garam masala * |
| 1 tbsp red chilli powder |
| ½ tsp fresh-ground black pepper |
| 1 tsp black cumin seeds *, roasted, ground |
| 1 tbsp ground coriander seeds |

(*Ingredients marked with an asterisk* can be found in Indian shops.)

Mix all the ingredients together except the egg, coriander and ghee. Leave for 30 minutes, then add the egg and coriander. Knead the mixture until it is sticky then divide into 18 portions and form into sausage shapes. Thread these onto skewers.

Cook over a medium-hot fire for about 20 minutes. Melt the ghee in a bowl on the side of the grill and baste with this. Seekh kebabs are normally served garnished with tomato and chopped onion, with lemon wedges for squeezing, as appetizers.

## Satay

Satay is one of the glories of barbecued appetizers. Satay is quite time-consuming to prepare, and each skewer contains very little meat, but it is so delicious that it is well worth the effort. It is impossible to give quantities – people will eat satay as long as it is available, and still look for more – but to allow less than three or four skewers per person is sheer cruelty. The secret of the taste lies in the marinades and the peanut sauce.

The meat is usually of high quality, and very carefully trimmed: possibilities include steak (especially sirloin, and even fillet / filet), lamb (especially leg), chicken (breast for preference), pork (any lean cut), firm-fleshed fish and shrimp.

For meat or fish satay, cut the meat into ½ in (12 mm) cubes and thread on bamboo skewers that have been soaked for at least 1 hour in water – for shrimp, use fair-size tails (frozen will do). Marinate the skewers for at least 1 hour, turning occasionally.

PORK MARINADE 4 tbsp oil, 4 tbsp soy sauce, 3 tbsp honey, 2 tbsp vinegar, 1 tsp aniseed, 2 cloves of garlic (crushed), salt and fresh-ground black pepper to taste. Squeeze a piece of very fresh root ginger in a garlic press to get a little ginger juice for an additional, tangy ginger flavour.

LAMB MARINADE In an electric blender, purée an onion with 4 tbsp each of peanut oil and soy sauce, plus salt and pepper to taste.

BEEF MARINADE Dilute ½ tsp pure tamarind extract (try oriental stores) in 2 tbsp water. Add the juice of half a lemon, 4 tbsp soy sauce, 1 tsp sugar, 3 cloves of garlic (crushed) and one grated or puréed onion. Again, add salt and pepper to taste.

CHICKEN MARINADE (1) 4 tbsp soy sauce, 1 tbsp honey, 2 tbsp ginger juice (see pork marinade, above), 2 tbsp dry sherry, salt, and either fresh ground black pepper or chilli powder.

CHICKEN MARINADE (2) Dissolve ⅓ cup / 85 g / 3 oz of cream of coconut in ⅔ cup / 150 ml / 6 fl oz of hot water, and then beat the mixture to a thick cream. Add 1 tsp pure tamarind extract, 1 tbsp ground coriander, 1 tbsp dried fennel, 2 tsp cumin, 2 tsp ground cinnamon, ¾ tsp turmeric, the seeds of 3 white or green cardamoms, nutmeg and chilli to taste. Beat well, then add 1 onion (grated or chopped in a food processor or liquidizer), 1 tbsp ginger juice, and 2 cloves crushed garlic.

SEAFOOD MARINADE (1) 5 tbsp soy sauce, 1 tbsp ginger juice, 3 tbsp dry sherry; pepper and salt.

SEAFOOD MARINADE (2) For a hotter, spicier version of the above, add two crushed cloves of garlic and two (or more) chopped hot green chillies.

SEAFOOD MARINADE (3) Add 2 tbsp each of vinegar and honey to either of the above recipes for a sweet-and-sour taste.

SEAFOOD MARINADE (4) Dissolve ¼ cup / 60 gm / 2 oz cream of coconut in ⅓ cup / 75 ml / 3 fl oz hot water. Liquidize with 1 small onion, 1 clove of garlic, 2 small fresh hot chillies, and the grated zest of about half a lemon. Add salt and freshly-ground black pepper to taste.

SEAFOOD MARINADE (5) Dissolve 1 tsp tamarind extract in 5 tbsp water. Add an equal quantity of peanut oil or sesame oil, plus salt and pepper to taste.

## PEANUT SAUCE

### PART 1

| |
| --- |
| *2 medium onions* |
| *4–6 garlic cloves* |
| *4 fresh hot chillies* |
| *1 tbsp shrimp paste (from oriental shops)* |
| *2 tsp ground coriander* |
| *2 tsp ground cumin* |
| *1 tsp dried fennel* |
| *4 tbsp peanut oil for frying* |

### PART 2

| |
| --- |
| *¾ cup / 180 g / 6 oz creamed coconut* |
| *1 cup / 225 ml / 8 fl oz water* |
| *2 tsp tamarind extract* |
| *2 tbsp ginger juice* |
| *2 tbsp sugar* |
| *1½ cups / 350 g / 12 oz crunchy peanut butter* |
| *juice of 1 lime* |
| *grated zest of 1 lemon* |
| *salt, freshly-ground black pepper* |

Proportions may be varied widely to suit individual tastes: in particular, the number of chillies may be halved, doubled or even tripled; and the quantities of garlic, shrimp paste, soy sauce and sugar may be increased by 50–100 per cent.

Dissolve the cream of coconut in the water, in a saucepan or using a microwave oven. Dissolve the tamarind extract in 3–4 tbsp of water.

In a blender, liquidizer or food processor, purée together all of the ingredients for Part 1 except the oil. Fry the paste in the oil until it is strongly aromatic. Then add all the ingredients from Part 2 with enough water to make it thin enough to stir easily. Heat, and simmer gently for up to 10 minutes, by which time the sauce should be thick and creamy (with grains) like a Dijon mustard. Reheat in the microwave, or in a pot on the barbecue to serve.

## Seafood Kebabs

Because most kinds of seafood cook faster than meat, it is often possible to make garnished kebabs with olives, tomatoes and onions, on the skewer along with the fish or shellfish. Here are some examples:

### PRAWN KEBABS

| SERVES 4 (as an appetizer) |
| --- |
| *1 lb / 450 g / 1 lb fresh prawns* |
| *¼ cup / 55 ml / 2 fl oz melted butter* |
| *¼ cup / 55 ml / 2 fl oz lemon juice* |
| *6–8 rashers bacon* |

Combine the melted butter and lemon juice, to use as a basting sauce.

Shell the prawns, and remove the veins. Remove the rind from the bacon and cut each rasher into halves or thirds – a piece big enough to wrap each prawn, which is then threaded onto a skewer.

Cook over medium to hot coals until the prawns are cooked and the bacon is crisp, about 10–15 minutes. Turn and baste frequently; baste again just before serving, and serve any remaining butter-lemon mixture as a sauce.

ABOVE Push shrimps close together on skewers.

Allow clams (and other shellfish) to open of their own accord; then they are ready to eat.

## FISH AND FRUIT KEBABS

SERVES  4 – 6  (as an appetizer)

¼ cup / 55 ml / 2 fl oz melted butter

¼ cup / 55 ml / 2 fl oz lemon juice

¾ lb / 350 g / ¾ lb white fish

3 large bananas

Make a basting sauce of butter and lemon juice as for the prawn-and-bacon kebab.

Fish and peaches or bananas make a surprisingly good combination. Choose any firm-fleshed white fish; cut into cubes about 1 in (2.5 cm) on a side. Alternate fish and slices of banana or wedges of peach, and cook for 15–20 minutes over hot coals. Turn and baste frequently, and serve the remaining butter/lemon mixture as a sauce.

## LOBSTER-PRAWN-SCALLOP KEBABS

SERVES  4

¼ cup / 60 g / 2 fl oz melted butter

2 tbsp lemon juice

1 small lobster, about 2 lb / 900 g

½ lb / 225 g / ½ lb fresh prawns

½ lb / 225 g / ½ lb shelled fresh scallops

24 cherry tomatoes

24 large stuffed green olives

2 tbsp fresh parsley, chopped finely

salt and pepper to taste

Combine the melted butter and the lemon juice as a brushing sauce.

Remove the meat from the tail of the lobster, and cut into chunks. Shell the prawns, and remove the veins. Alternate the ingredients on the skewers and sprinkle with salt and pepper.

Barbecue over medium–low heat for 10–15 minutes, turning and basting frequently. Sprinkle with parsley, and serve with the remaining lemon butter, salad and garlic bread as a main course or as an appetizer before steak.

## FISH STEAKS

While whole fish may appeal to the traditionalist and to the true fish lover, fish fillets and fish steaks are easier to cook and contain few or no bones.

The best fillets and steaks to barbecue are from firm-fleshed fish: tuna, shark and swordfish are particularly delicious, especially if they are not overcooked. Halibut and salmon are good, and cod tastes better this way although it sometimes tends to fall apart. Fillets and steaks should be at least 1 in (2.5 cm) and preferably 1½ in (4 cm) thick or they will dry out, as well as being more likely to fall apart.

Marinate the fish for half an hour or so in lemon juice and olive oil (one part lemon juice to two parts oil), with chopped parsley or tarragon, and pepper and salt to taste. Coat with flour if you want a crispy crust, although this is optional. Cook over a low heat for 1–4 minutes per side, depending on your tastes, the thickness of the steak, and the kind of fish used.

## *Fish in Foil*

While cooking fish in foil may offend purists, there is no doubt that if offers many advantages, not least that the fish won't fall apart or stick to the barbecue.

## POACHED FISH FILLETS

### S E R V E S   4

*4 fish fillets, about 6 oz / 180 g each*

*2 tbsp melted butter*

*2 tbsp lemon juice or dry white wine (or a mixture of both)*

*1 tbsp fresh parsley, chopped*

*salt and pepper*

Measure the thickness of the fillets at their thickest point. This determines the cooking time: allow 12–15 minutes per in, 5–6 minutes per cm.

To make a parcel, put a sheet of foil about 18 in (50 cm) square on a plate and make a depression in the centre so the liquid does not run out. Lay the fillets side by side (if they overlap, it will spoil your estimate of cooking time), making more than one parcel if you have too many fillets to fit in without overlapping.

Add the butter and lemon juice/wine and season with salt, pepper and parsley. Fold the foil over the top to create a baggy enclosure. Cook over medium-hot coals.

BELOW Some fish fillets (such as thresher shark, LEFT) may be cooked on the grill; others are best 'poached' in a foil parcel, such as bass fillets (BELOW).

ABOVE When barbecuing salmon, it is best to cook it in a foil 'cradle', which keeps it moist and prevents the cooked fish from breaking when you pick it up.

## GRILLED SALMON IN FOIL

### SERVES 4

$2^{1}/_{2}$–3 lb / 1.25–1.5 kg / $2^{1}/_{2}$–3 lb whole salmon, cleaned weight

juice of 1 lemon

1 tbsp olive oil

salt and pepper

$^{1}/_{4}$ cup / 30–40 g / 1–$1^{1}/_{2}$ oz fresh dill, chopped

$^{1}/_{4}$ cup / 60 g / 2 oz butter

Dijon mustard

oil or butter to grease foil

lemon wedges

The foil is used as a cradle, rather than as a wrap. It should be long enough to cradle the whole fish, with a bit at either end for ease in handling. Grease the foil thickly with butter (or brush it all over with olive oil) to prevent sticking, and poke holes in it with a skewer so that the smoke can reach the fish.

Season the fish inside and out with lemon juice, olive oil, salt and pepper. Put three or four sprigs of dill in the cavity and place the fish on the foil. Leave to stand for 20 minutes for the flavours to mingle.

Cook over a hot fire. After five minutes, *carefully* turn the fish in the foil cradle, and repeat at 5-minute intervals. The fish should be cooked in 20–30 minutes in total, depending on how you like your salmon.

Beat together the chopped dill, the butter (soften it in the microwave) and the mustard (add more to taste); this, and the lemon wedges, accompany the fish. Rather than trying to lift it out of the foil when it is cooked, just roll it onto the serving platter.

## SHELLFISH

Shrimp and mussels can both be cooked in foil packets. Scrub small mussels and remove the beards, and remove the heads and legs from shrimps or prawns. Cook either type of shellfish in batches of half a dozen, forming a single layer in a foil pouch. Before sealing each pouch, add a knob (say 2 tbsp) of garlic butter.

Shrimp should be cooked over medium heat, and will be ready in 10–12 minutes. Cook mussels over medium-high heat, shaking the bundle every minute or two: they are cooked when open.

Pork ribs, popular in Chinese cooking, are one of the classic American barbecue foods, and come in three types:

SPARE RIBS are cut from just behind the pork shoulder. A full set of ribs is a long, triangular cut made up of bone, cartilage, and a thin layer of meat which can be cooked to a crisp. Although some people regard them as awkward to cook and messy to eat, others rank them second to none in barbecue delicacies.

BACK RIBS are shorter and neater to eat, but have (if anything) even less meat.

COUNTRY-STYLE RIBS are cut from the loin, and have very much more meat than the other two cuts.

Many people pre-cook ribs before barbecuing them, which cuts down the time on the grill considerably. If you start with raw ribs, you can reckon on a minimum of 1 hour, with 1½ hours a realistic maximum. If they are pre-cooked, you can reckon on ½–1 hour on the grill over a medium-low heat for ribs of all kinds. A drip pan will reduce the chance of flare-ups.

To pre-cook ribs, you can bake them in a foil packet on a hot grill for ¾–1 hour; steam them in a saucepan on the stove; or simply boil them. Plain boiling is surprisingly good for country-style ribs, which can be boiled until they are falling-apart tender, then crisped magnificently on a grill.

A whole rack of spare ribs is most easily cooked in one piece as cutting smaller pieces makes handling more difficult. You can also skewer them accordion-style on a spit if you want to cook them on a rotisserie.

Baby back ribs can be cooked directly on the grill, or (cut into servings of four ribs each) in a tumble basket, while country-style ribs may be cooked on a rack in a closed barbecue, or simply cooked directly on the grill.

Do not baste with thick barbecue sauces until 15 minutes or so before the meat is finally cooked, or the sauce will simply burn. Either cook the ribs without any basting, or use a thin marinade sauce and use that to baste .

Determining quantities for ribs (in terms of weight of meat per person) is all but impossible: it depends very much upon the quality of the ribs, the quality of the cooking, and the hunger (or gluttony) of the diners. As a very rough guess, allow ½–1 lb / 225–450 g of ribs per person – you will need fewer of the meatier country-style ribs, but many a gourmand can demolish more than 2 lb / 900 g of spare ribs without really trying.

The traditional accompaniments for ribs are beer, beans , garlic bread and salad

BELOW Baby back pork ribs tend to give the least meat of all ribs but are still great fun to chew on.

LEFT If you want ribs with a maximum amount of meat, then choose country-style pork ribs.

## Beef Ribs

Traditionally, Texans ate beef ribs instead of pork ribs. This was partly a question of availability, and partly because beef ribs are bigger than pork ribs, everything being bigger in Texas.

Outside Texas, however, beef ribs for barbecue are not always easy to find. You may have either to cultivate a butcher, or to buy a standing rib roast and remove the rib eye (for rib eye steaks!) yourself. You will need two sharp knives for this, one large butcher's knife and one small boning knife. You will also need practice and care.

Although you can use almost any barbecue sauce on ribs, some people prefer to eat them on their own, and others prefer to serve them with grainy Dijon or old-fashioned mustard.

Allow 2 to 3 rib bones per person, up to about 1 lb / 450 g in uncooked weight. Pre-cooking beef ribs is less important than with pork as many people prefer their beef rare.

## RARE, CRUSTY RIBS

Over a medium-hot fire, brown the ribs first on one side, then on the other – at least 5 minutes on each side. When they are browned, brush with barbecue sauce or Dijon mustard, or simply continue to cook for another 5–10 minutes a side. This gives you rich, crusty ribs with rare meat sticking to them. They will not, however, be particularly tender: you can rely on getting a lot of meat stuck in your front teeth as you gnaw the bones.

## WELL-DONE RIBS

Wrap the ribs in heavy-duty foil, and bake over a high direct heat for an hour. This will render out some of the fat, but (more importantly) it will ensure moist, tender, well-cooked meat on the inside.

Pour off the fat, and continue to cook over a medium-low indirect heat for at least 15 minutes on each side (or 30 minutes on a rack) using a covered barbecue. If you turn only once, you can coat the ribs liberally with barbecue sauce when you start this stage, without much risk of burning. Heat some extra sauce in a pan at the side of the grill, to serve with the meat.

This is the best way to cook beef ribs if you are a barbecue sauce addict. Serve with beer, beans, garlic bread and salsa .

ABOVE Beef ribs are traditionally Texan, and may not be easy to find. However, it is always worth asking your butcher.

# Fajitas

A *fajita* is a cut of beef (not a method of cooking, as sometimes thought), but opinions as to where *'fajitas'* are cut from varies. Generally, though, it is accepted that they are cut from the area of the diaphragm, and are tough and fibrous with a layer of gristly membrane and a lot of fat. They therefore require careful stripping and tenderizing before cooking, which either the butcher will do for you, or which you can do at home.

Originally a Tex-Mex field-hands' dish from the border country (hence the cheapness of the cut, which is also known as skirt steak), but the sudden popularity of the dish in the 1980s means that it is now often cheaper to marinate and cook *'fajita*-style' dishes using other cuts of meat.

To prepare real *fajitas,* lay the meat on a cutting board and carefully remove the fat with a very sharp knife. Next, remove the tough outer membrane by holding the steak while you slice away the membrane. And finally, puncture the meat repeatedly with a sharp, pointed knife, working both with the grain and against it. Using a fork to puncture the meat with too will help the marinades to enter. Do not use a meat mallet or bottled tenderizer, or the meat will be reduced to pulp.

If you are preparing other cuts *'fajita*-style', you are saved much of this effort. Flank steak probably comes closest in flavour, but it must be sliced as soon as you take if off the grill or it will rapidly become very tough and leathery.

Marinate the meat for at least 4 hours, and preferably overnight, the *fajita* marinades below or your own marinade. The usual rules apply: papaya and pineapple juice tenderize the most and fastest, citrus juices are next, and then comes wines and beers or other liquids. Other ingredients are just for flavouring.

## MARGARITA MARINADE

| |
|---|
| *½ cup / 110 ml / 4 fl oz Tequila* |
| *¾ cup / 170 ml / 6 fl oz lime juice* |
| *¼ cup / 55 ml / 2 fl oz Triple Sec* |

## LIME MARINADE

| |
|---|
| *1 cup / 225 ml / 8 fl oz beef stock (broth)* |
| *3 tbsp Worcestershire sauce* |
| *1–2 garlic cloves, finely chopped* |
| *1 tbsp chopped fresh coriander* |
| *juice of 1 lime* |

To serve *fajitas* as a steak (which used to be quite common), barbecue the meat over a medium heat for 6–8 minutes on each side. Brush with marinade while cooking, and just before serving.

To serve with *tortillas,* cook as above and then slice diagonally into thin strips about 4 inches (10 cm) long. Heat large flour *tortillas* on the grill, and have the following garnishes available for those who want to make up their own *burritos.* If *tortillas* are a problem, use chapattis or pita bread instead.

## GARNISHES FOR FAJITA BURRITOS

sour cream
salsa
guacamole or sliced avocado
bell peppers, raw, lightly fried or grilled
raw onion, thinly sliced
sliced tomato
shredded lettuce
refried beans

Although barbecuing seems to be the meat-eater's domain, there are many ways of cooking vegetables with a barbecue. They fall into four groups, namely: cooking on the grill; cooking kebabs; cooking in the embers; and various methods which include steaming in foil.

## Grilled Corn

There are two ways to grill corn: with the husk and without. Grilling with the husk gives a tender, juicier ear, but grilling without results in a flavour and texture all its own.

To cook with the husk, first remove the silk (the threads between the husk and the corn). This means peeling back the husk without removing it, so do it as carefully as possible. Yo may need to secure the husk with florists' wire (but *not* the plastic-coated kind!) when you replace it.

Then soak the corn in ice-water for at least 30 minutes – this chills and saturates it – and then roast it over a medium, direct fire for about 20 minutes, turning frequently. To check if the corn is cooked, prick a kernel with a knife; if it spurts clear juice it is done.

Parched corn (cooked without the husk) is a roadside food in many countries, from Mexico to India. In Mexico, they usually parboil it first; in India, as in Morocco, it is just grilled.

To parboil, bring a large kettle or saucepan of water to the boil, and plunge the ears of corn into it for no more than a couple of minutes. Then finish cooking the corn on a medium or medium-hot grill for another 3–5 minutes, depending on the heat, turning frequently.

For plain grilled corn, use a low heat for 10–20 minutes. Once again, turn frequently. Try serving plain with salt (no butter).

## Grilled Spring Onions

Spring onions, green onions, ciboes, chipples, *cebollitas* – whatever you call them, they are surprisingly good grilled. Spread them ½–1 in (12–25 mm) apart and cook them over a medium heat until they are soft, wilted, and golden-brown: at least 10–12 minutes. Allow three or four onions per person.

## Grilled Carrots

Parboil carrots until they are about half cooked (about 3–4 minutes), then finish cooking over a medium heat, turning frequently and basting with butter. Most people prefer their barbecued carrots to be slightly crunchy. Sprinkle a pinch of parsley over the carrots before serving. 1 lb / 450 gm of carrots should serve four as a side dish.

## Grilled Potatoes

Whole potatoes can very successfully be cooked on the grill. Small potatoes (as well as sweet potatoes and Jerusalem artichokes) require 45–60 minutes; larger 'baking' potatoes take 1–1½ hours. Turn them every 15 minutes or so until the potatoes can be easily pierced with a fork.

If you want a soft skin, oil the potato well before you put it on the grill: for a crisp skin, forget the oil.

Alternatively, cut large potatoes in thick, fairly uniform slices of about ½ in (12 mm) and cook over a medium-to-hot fire. Baste repeatedly with melted butter, turning frequently. The potatoes should be golden and cooked in around 20 minutes. One large potato per person is adequate, but (as with so much barbecue food), many people may want more!

For a variation on this last recipe, crush a clove of garlic into a little pan of melted butter at the side of the grill and use for basting.

## Cooking with a Grill Basket

A surprising number of vegetables can be cooked in a grill basket. Oil the basket to prevent them sticking and brush the vegetables liberally with melted butter

ABOVE A selection of vegetables that can be barbecued: corn, potato, carrots, spring onions and pineapple slices.

or olive oil; turn frequently while cooking. Courgettes (zucchini) can be cooked this way, as can summer squash (halved) and even thickly-sliced aubergines (egg-plant).

## Vegetable Kebabs

Cooking both meat and vegetables on the same skewer is possible, but risky: all too often, the meat will still be half-raw when the vegetables are either burning or falling apart. A much better idea is to grill vegetable kebabs separately.

If you are using any vegetables which are notoriously slow-cooking, such as carrots, it is a good idea to parboil them first. Only experience will teach you exactly what sizes to cut the various vegetables that can be cooked on a skewer, but you might care to try this all-and-everything recipe to compare as many types of vegetables as possible:

### MIXED VEGETABLE KEBAB

| SERVES 8 |
| --- |
| ¾ lb / 350 g / ¾ lb yellow summer squash |
| 1 large purple aubergine (eggplant) |
| ¾ lb / 350 g / ¾ lb courgettes |
| 4 bell peppers, red, green or yellow |
| 4 medium onions |
| 12 cherry tomatoes |
| ½ cup / 110 ml / 4 fl oz olive oil |
| ¼ cup / 55 ml / 2 fl oz cider or wine vinegar |
| 1 tsp dried basil |
| ½ tsp dried thyme |
| 2 tbsp chopped fresh parsley |

Squashes are less common in Britain than in the United States, but the hook-shaped yellow summer squash is reasonably widely available. Very tender young pumpkins can also be cooked the same way.

Cut the squash into 1 in (2.5 cm) cubes or slices, the aubergine into 1 in (2.5 cm) cubes and the courgettes into 1 in (2.5 cm) slices. Seed and core the peppers, and cut into squares of the same size. Peel the onions and cut into quarters.

Marinade all the vegetables in the oil / vinegar /

herb mixture: a plastic self-seal bag is the easiest container to use. Shake or roll the bag occasionally to ensure even coating, but be careful to avoid breaking up the onions.

Then thread the vegetables onto a skewer, alternating the types. Cook over medium coals, turning frequently and basting with marinade, for 10–15 minutes. By this time they should be cooked, though the tomatoes will be very soft indeed.

If you want to add carrots, parboil them for about 3–4 minutes or they may be excessively crunchy for some people's tastes. Likewise, mushrooms should be steamed for a couple of minutes, or there is a real danger that they will split and fall off the skewer.

ABOVE Ready for a vegetable kebab: onions, tomatoes, mushrooms, courgettes (zucchini) and peppers.

BELOW Squash and aubergine are also good for barbecued vegetable kebabs.

## Vegetables in the Embers

Scouts of both sexes will certainly remember baking potatoes in the embers of a fire – and then trying to eat the charred, gritty, half-raw result!

The technique *can* be made to work, though, and to work deliciously. You need rather more patience than you had as a child, and you need the air-vent shut right down and (preferably) the top closed on a covered barbecue, so that the embers smoulder at as low a temperature as possible.

### POTATOES COOKED IN THE EMBERS

Potatoes are the obvious choice for ember cooking. If you are not planning to use foil, oil the skin to reduce charring. A medium-sized potato should take something between ¾–1 hour to cook fully. Turn often, using tongs.

The potatoes will require far less attention if you wrap them in foil before putting them in the embers but somehow, it isn't the same. They will take 5–10 minutes longer to cook, too.

### SQUASH COOKED IN THE EMBERS

A less obvious choice, but arguably even more effective, is cooking hard-shelled winter squashes in the embers. Oil the outside, slash the skin *deeply* (to avoid the risk of explosion), and (once again) turn frequently during a cooking time of 45–60 minutes.

### ONIONS COOKED IN THE SKIN

The real surprise, at least until you try it, is onions cooked in the embers. Use large, sweet onions such as Bermuda, Spanish or Vidalia onions. Cut off the ends (which would otherwise burn), but do not peel them: just put them snugly into the embers and leave them for about 45 minutes, turning fairly frequently. The outer skin will be blackened and inedible and should be thrown away, but the onion inside is delicious.

### OTHER VEGETABLES IN EMBERS

You can cook almost any vegetable in this way, but you would be well advised to wrap it in heavy-duty foil first. With more delicate vegetables, such as courgettes (zucchini), use a double layer of foil to reduce the risk of charring. Corn will cook in the embers in 35–45 minutes; courgettes, individually wrapped, in 30–40 minutes; and mushrooms, with butter, in about 30–60 minutes, depending on the size of the parcel.

## Other Ways to Cook Vegetables

Many vegetables can be cooked in a foil wrap on the grill, others with only a partial foil covering. Potatoes and squashes, for example, can be halved, the cut side protected with foil, and then cooked on the grill. A recipe for German potato salad is also given here; it's not barbecued at all, but still belongs in a barbecue book because it goes so well with food cooked in this way.

### HALVED VEGETABLES

Cutting potatoes and summer squash in half, lengthwise, makes it easier to cook them evenly all the way through. Protecting the cut side with aluminium foil not only promotes moistness and prevents charring; it also slows down the rate of heat transfer, as the foil reflects a good deal of the heat, and makes even cooking easier, if longer. For either potatoes or winter squash, the cooking time is about 60 minutes. Begin with the foil side downwards but after 35–40 minutes, turn and cook the uncovered side for the remaining time. The foil can be removed when you turn the vegetables over.

### GRILLED MUSHROOMS

| SERVES 4 |
| --- |
| *1 lb / 450 g / 1 lb mushrooms* |
| *¼ cup / 60 g / 2 oz butter* |
| *salt and pepper* |

Wash and trim the mushrooms, and if they are really big, slice them. Divide the prepared mushrooms into four portions and place each on a large piece of doubled aluminium foil. Dot the mushrooms in each parcel with 1 tbsp / ½ oz / 15 g butter, and season to taste. Wrap the parcels securely and barbecue over hot coals for at least 15 minutes, turning every 5 minutes or so. The mushrooms are cooked when they are tender, but a little overcooking (even 5–10 minutes) will do no harm.

There are only a few recipes in this book which are not actually cooked on the barbecue: German potato salad was one, and beans and salsa are two more. Both of these are inseparably associated with Californian, Texan and New Mexico barbecues. Salsa (Spanish for sauce) usually refers to a mixture of tomatoes, onions and other ingredients, served cold; and the classic beans served with a barbecue are Santa Maria-style.

## SANTA MARIA-STYLE BEANS

### SERVES 8 AS A SIDE DISH

| |
|---|
| 1 lb / 450 gm / 1 lb dried beans |
| 1 fresh hot green chilli (serrano) |
| 1 bay leaf |
| 1 tbsp olive oil or lard |
| 4 tbsp tomato purée |
| 1 tbsp mild chilli powder |
| ¼ lb / 110 g / ¼ lb bacon |
| 1 garlic clove, finely chopped |
| 1 small onion, finely chopped (optional) |

For true Santa Maria style, the beans should be *pinquitos*, but small dried haricots will serve as well. Likewise, the chilli powder should be *pasilla* or *Nuevo Mexico*, but any mild chilli powder will do.

Chop the fresh hot chilli (*serrano* or *jalapeño*) very finely. Sort the beans to remove any stones, and wash them carefully but do not soak them. Cover with plenty of water, add the chopped chilli and the bay leaf, and bring to the boil. DO NOT SALT as this will toughen the beans. Simmer gently, adding more water as necessary. When the bean skins begin to wrinkle, add the olive oil and continue to cook until the beans are soft (this can take several hours). When they are, add salt to taste and cook for another 30 minutes without adding any more water: these beans are not drained.

Dice the bacon finely, and fry gently until it begins to render its own fat. Continue until the bacon is crisp, and then fry the garlic and the onion (if used) until soft. Add the beans, tomato purée and chilli powder, mix well and simmer (preferably in a pan at the side of a covered barbecue) until serving. Stir occasionally to help the barbecue flavour to permeate the beans.

These beans can be frozen in heavy plastic bags, thawed naturally or in a microwave, and then reheated on the barbecue.

ABOVE Salsa is quickly made, beans take longer; both are delicious and popular at barbecues.

## SALSA

### SERVES 8 AS A SIDE DISH

| |
|---|
| 28 oz / 800 g / 28 oz can of tomatoes |
| 1 medium red onion, finely chopped |
| handful fresh coriander, chopped |
| 1–3 fresh hot chilli peppers |
| 1–3 garlic cloves, finely chopped |
| 1 tbsp olive oil (optional) |
| 1 tbsp wine vinegar (optional) |
| ½ tsp dried oregano |

Quantities can be varied: coriander, in particular, can range from a couple of tablespoons to a large handful. If you grow your own coriander, crush a few unripe coriander seeds under a heavy knife-blade for a superb aromatic flavour.

Empty the tomatoes, undrained, into a large bowl. Add all the other ingredients, and mix together with your hand – not a very scientific procedure, but definitely the most effective. Leave for at least 30 minutes for the flavours to blend: 2–3 hours or more is even better.

Use as a dip with corn chips, or spoon over beans, steak, hamburgers or anything else.

# Breads

Of the many breads you can serve with a barbecue, garlic bread is probably the most popular. But you can also serve pita bread from the Near and Middle East; *nan* and *chapattis* from India; Mexican tortillas; or even bread cooked right on the barbecue. Keep cooked bread warm by wrapping it in a tea-towel and leaving it at the edge of the barbecue.

## GARLIC BREAD

Take a large French loaf and cut it almost through at intervals of ¾–1½ in (2–4 cm). Spread softened garlic butter between the slices and wrap the loaf in foil. Grill for 20 minutes over medium-hot

coals and for the last few minutes, uncover the top of the bread to ensure a crisp, crusty finish. As a variation, try pounding two or three anchovy fillets into the garlic butter, and omit the parsley.

## PITA BREAD

Pita (or pitta) bread is a flat, oval sheet of bread eaten throughout Greece and in the Near and Middle East. Available in most large supermarkets, it is at its best re-heated over a charcoal grill: it should balloon out, making the pocket in the middle easier to fill. Give it 15–30 seconds on each side over medium-hot coals. Neither time nor temperature is particularly important, so long as you do not burn it.

## NAN

Nan is an Indian bread which looks like pita, but tastes rather different and rarely develops a pocket: this is a mopping-up and dipping bread, rather than

a bread for holding food. Reheat as for pita, or brush with garlic butter for an additional flavour.

## PARATHAS

If you live near an Indian shop, you may be able to buy parathas – rich, buttered flat bread that is cooked by frying. Quickly re-heating over charcoal gives a delicious flavour and makes for a very different accompaniment to barbecued food.

## TORTILLAS AND CHAPATTIS

These are both thin, unleavened breads. Flour tortillas are very much like chapattis, while corn tortillas have their own flavour. All are delicious when re-heated on charcoal. Heat each side for 5–10 seconds.

## BAKED BREAD

Conventional bread recipes, including frozen ready-made breads or corn-bread made from a mix, can be cooked on a covered barbecue using indirect heat. Putting the bread over a drip pan, or an area cleared of coals, prevents the bottom of the bread from burning. Approximate cooking times are as follows:

Pan loaf, 1 lb / 450 g   Medium, 15–20 minutes
Rolls, in baking pan   Medium / low, 15–20 minutes
Corn bread   Medium, about 35 minutes

With a covered barbecue and medium, indirect heat you can cook other baked delicacies such as gingerbread, although it is disputable whether this is a better idea than baking in the oven.

BELOW Flour and corn tortillas.

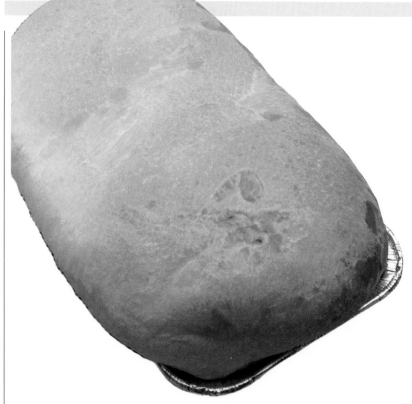

ABOVE A conventional loaf can be baked in a covered barbecue.

## Salads

Salads are a natural accompaniment for barbecued food, giving a welcome contrast in temperature and texture. Because a barbecue is a usually fairly long-drawn-out affair compared to a conventional meal, it is a good idea to make salads which will not dry out or wilt unduly. This is why a cabbage salad is a good idea, or one made with a heavier lettuce, such as Romaine or Iceberg.

### CABBAGE SALAD

#### SERVES ABOUT 6

*To half a head of cabbage, shredded, add any or all of the following:*

*Almonds, whole or sliced, small handful*

*Avocado(s), diced*

*Beetroot (beet), sliced*

*Carrot, shredded*

*Celery, one or two sticks, sliced*

*Cheese, 1/4 lb / 4 oz / 110 g, diced*

*Coriander, chopped, up to a handful*

*Raisins, small handful*

*Red onion, thinly sliced*

*Tomatoes, sliced*

*Walnuts, 1–2 tbsp*

Toss together with a dressing made of two parts olive oil to one part lime or lemon juice. Instead of lemon juice alone, you may care to use half lemon juice, half vinegar.

RIGHT Cabbage salad provides a refreshing contrast to barbecue food and can be varied almost endlessly according to taste.